"His Majes*: elo-*
quence, the passi *imate*
relationship with *est of*
life's trials.

Ms. Peggy Clemons presents an exquisitely written, fresh and delightfully engaging read, that is both a personal GPS for our lives and an incredible resource for Bible scholars of every level. It takes you on a journey; a quest, to broaden your understanding of God's Word and the incredible life and power within it, every verse, every story, personal and potent.

I have had the honor to walk with Ms. Peggy for long enough to greatly respect and love the woman that she is, all that she has achieved, and her incredible relationship with her Creator. I highly recommend this to all who wish to follow in her footsteps.

Much love,

—**Jane Evans**
Senior Global Pastor, Influencers Church, Duluth, Georgia

"His Majesty's Heavenly GPS" is a great read, wonderfully written, mapped out by the language of wisdom, vibrant and full of suggestions the Spirit of God has given to us through the writing of Peggy Clemons.

In reading this book, you will see how the Holy Spirit has given the author insight for us to consider; from the beginning, his ways of doing things were right from the start. God made known to us that in the last days knowledge would increase. Those days are here, and we are moving into higher realms of understandings that are much needed.

The importance of this book is to give us greater insight on how to use God's Word and move us towards a deeper understanding on getting to know him better. This will produce high confidence, as you pay attention to each word and flow with what the Lord is saying to the Church. While taking this journey, you will see descriptive messages [for example—On God's Interstate G 45:9-28 - This book will cause you to see descriptive instructions that tell you to turn right on Restoration Road, proceed on Restoration Road to Jacob Road]. Have a good read!

—**Apostle/Prophet, Carmen Michelle Johnson**

To God Be the Glory —

Much Love
Dr. Peggy

02/22

His Majesty's Heavenly GPS

Directions for Divine Destiny

PEGGY CLEMONS
FOREWORD BY DR. CINDY TRIMM

Copyright © 2019 by Peggy Clemons
ISBN: 978-1-949297-19-5
LCCN:2019915665

All rights reserved. No part of this book may be reproduced, stored in a retrieval system, or transmitted in any form or by any means--electronic, mechanical, digital, photocopy, or any other---without prior permission from the publisher and author, except as provided by the United States of America copyright law.

Unless otherwise noted, all scriptures are from THE MESSAGE: THE BIBLE IN CONTEMPORARY ENGLISH, Copyright©1993, 1994, 1995, 1996, 2000, 2001, 2002. Used by permission of NavPress Publishing Group.

Please note that "The Message" is not a literal translation of the Bible; instead, it is a highly idiomatic, personal paraphrase by Eugene H. Peterson.

Scripture quotations marked (AMP) are taken from the AMPLIFIED® BIBLE, Copyright© 1954, 1958, 1962, 1964, 1965, 1987 by the Lockman Foundation Used by Permission. (www.Lockman.org)

Scripture quotations marked (ESV) are taken from THE HOLY BIBLE, ENGLISH STANDARD VERSION®, Copyright© 2001 by Crossway, a publishing ministry of Good News Publishers. Used by permission.

Scripture quotations marked (NIV) are taken from THE HOLY BIBLE, NEW INTERNATIONAL VERSION®. Copyright© 1973, 1978, 1984, 2011 by Biblica, Inc.™. Used by permission of Zondervan

Scripture quotations marked (NKJV) are taken from the NEW KING JAMES VERSION®. Copyright© 1982 by Thomas Nelson, Inc. Used by permission. All rights reserved.

Scripture quotations marked (NLT) are taken from THE HOLY BIBLE, NEW LIVING TRANSLATION, Copyright© 1996, 2004, 2007 by Tyndale House Foundation. Used by permission of Tyndale House Publishers, Inc., Carol Stream, Illinois 60188. All rights reserved. Used by permission.

You may contact the author at: info@peggyclemons.com

Individuals and church groups may order books from Peggy Clemons directly, or from the publisher. Retailers and wholesalers should order from our distributors. Refer to the Deeper Revelation Books website for distribution information, as well as an online catalog of all our books.

Published by:
Deeper Revelation Books
Revealing "the deep things of God" (1 Cor. 2:10)
P.O. Box 4260 • Cleveland, TN 37320 • 423-478-2843
Website: *www.deeperrevelationbooks.org*
Email: *info@deeperrevelationbooks.org*

Deeper Revelation Books assists Christian authors in publishing and distributing their books. Final responsibility for design, content, permissions, editorial accuracy, and doctrinal views, either expressed or implied, belongs to the author.

Dedication

This book is dedicated to my Mom,

Virginia Brown Harvey, who has endured life's struggles, surpassed the opinions of men, trusted in the love, grace and mercy of her Heavenly Father, stood for morality, integrity and truth at all cost. My Mom, whose life pursuits set a standard of excellence, tenacity, persistence and honor endowed to her family and friends for generations to come.

My Mom, the orphan girl who would rise to be a woman of distinction, substance, character and prominence. A woman who understood the value of truth and loyalty. A woman of wealth and remarkable financial affluence, her motto being: "It's not how much money you make, but what you do with what you make." With her strong faith in God and extraordinary, exceptional work ethic, she literally owed no person anything but love.

My Mom, a living legacy who would climb the highest mountain to secure and show unconditional love to me, her daughter, her granddaughter, Chalet A. (Tranumn) Jean-Baptiste, her precious great-grandchildren, Ariana, Christopher and Elise, with the arsenal of her awe-inspiring, passionate wisdom, an endearing cloak of her love with deep, touching sacrifices of time, talent and treasure on every occasion and in every way.

To you, Mom,
My beloved, my hero, my confidant and dearest friend—
I Love, Appreciate and Adore You Immensely.
I Salute You!!!

Contents

Foreword 9

Introduction 11

An important Note 12

Chapter 1 / His Majesty's GPS 13

Chapter 2 / Genesis: Exquisite Peefection 17

Chapter 3 / Genesis: The Beginning 23

Chapter 4 / Genesis: The Power of First 29
    First Mentions & Scriptures 33

Chapter 5 / Genesis: The Marvel of Man 37

Chapter 6 / Genesis: The Meaning 41

Chapter 7 / The Heavenly GPS 43

Chapter 8 / Prologue to the
    GPS Coordinates 49

Chapter 9 / The Journey 61

Chapter 10 / Majestic Manual
    Heavenly GPS Coordinates 63

Chapter 11 / God Commanded the History
    of Creation 71

Royal Decrees 75

Royal Names 83

Acknowledgments 87

Endnotes 93

His Majesty's Heavenly GPS
Directions for Divine Destiny

ROYAL DECREE

Barricade the road that goes Nowhere;
Grace me with Your Clear Revelation.
I Choose the true road to Somewhere,
I post Your road signs at
Every curve and corner.
I grasp and cling to whatever
You tell me;
I'll run the course
You lay out for me
If you'll just show me how.

Psalms 119:29-32

FOREWORD

His Majesty's Heavenly GPS

If you have served God for any length of time, you've probably sought His will for your life in countless situations. You may have even felt like you were involved in a nearly impossible mission to find God's will or completely missed His direction. Maybe you are at a crossroad and need strategic insight as to which path to take.

Regardless of which scenario you identify with, the feeling that you've missed God's will is one of the most disappointing feelings for any believer. The truth is every believer's innermost being recognizes that learning to successfully find and follow God's will is the hallmark of a dynamic Christian life. You simply cannot thrive without it. Even more alarming is knowing that you missed or ignored God's will and now you are urgently trying to escape or repair the circumstances that were created as a result. No one wants to miss God's will, for to miss His will is to forfeit His greatest blessings and provisions.

The truth is many of us don't possess the necessary tools that allow for clarity and understanding for our Christian journey. As a result, we resign our lives to the guessing game that we desperately wish we knew how to avoid.

This doesn't have to be your story.

The Bible says that wisdom is crying aloud in the streets (Prov 8:1-3). In other words, God's will and all wise answers are not hard to locate.

His Majesty's Heavenly GPS is a roadmap and tool to finding God's divine direction in every circumstance of life.

Whatever the circumstances that brought you to this timely work I pray that you will find an invitation and an increasingly faithful response to the One whose purpose shapes your path, whose grace redeems your detours, whose power liberates you from the crippling bondages of the prior journey and whose transforming presence meets you at each turn in the road.

God wants you to rise above any confusion and learn how to peacefully find His divine direction. I have no doubt that by the time you're finished reading this book, that you will have received insight as you address issues that have been important to you and that you will be more confident about seeking God for solutions for your most pressing needs. Rest assured even if your situation is challenging, God is already working in your life and you are going to journey into His perfect will in spite of the myriad of challenges you face.

His Majesty's Heavenly GPS is a clarifying key to the path you should take in fulfilling your greater destiny. I believe that a greater understanding of God's vision for your life and your place in the Kingdom will be birthed as you devote your time to absorbing the long overdue and significant revelations within these priceless pages.

—**Dr. Cindy Trimm**
Life-Strategist, Author, Humanitarian

INTRODUCTION

The God of the Universe, the Master Creator, framed, fashioned and crafted heaven, earth and everything in them in "seven days," and then—the Omnipotent God time released it according to His plan and purpose.

Like the sun, moon, and stars which were assigned to mark seasons, days and years (especially on the fourth day of creation), this first universal clock set time in motion by the hand of an Omniscient (All-knowing) God. From the Antediluvian Age through the Information Age these periods of time remain suspended in the mind of God until His appointed time.

He has made everything beautiful and appropriate in its time. He has also planted eternity [a sense of divine purpose] in the human heart [a mysterious longing which nothing under the sun can satisfy, except God]—yet man cannot find out (comprehend, grasp) what God has done (His overall plan) from the beginning to the end.

Ecclesiastes 3:11 (AMP)

This perfect timing was decreed, spoken and written in a plan called—Life. And so, all the stories were penned in seven days from beginning to eternity and succinctly, specifically, magnificently, precisely and flawlessly time-released. Because of our human design, we are privileged to experience the space and time identified as our generation. Whatever life span we were chosen to experience, we have been especially equipped to function in excellence for that allotted portion of time, our chapter of life.

Our loving Creator wrote the book and stepped into it, orchestrating each paragraph and line. Join us to discover how His Majesty, King and Ruler of the heaven and earth designed it all, perfect and error-free. Follow along on the journey, as we sense how our own path, plan, purpose and undeniable destinies unfolded like the men in ancient times. How does our journey begin? How will we enrich our generation? Stroll down the road of mystery and the unknown boulevard filled with a course of events from present to future. As we navigate through the first recorded times in history, we ask ourrselves, "What's next for us?"

An Important Note

Eugene H. Peterson describes Genesis in *The Message Bible's* "Introduction to the Books of Moses" as a verbal witness to God's creative acts, God's intervening and gracious judgments. It also contains God's call to a life of faith and how God made covenants with us.

We are given a succession of stories with names of people, people who loved, believed and doubted, had children and married, experienced sin and grace.

If we pay attention, we find that we ourselves are living variations of these very stories. Adam and Eve, Cain and Abel, Noah and his sons, Abraham and Sarah, Isaac and Rebekah, Jacob and Rachel, Joseph and his brothers. The stories show clearly that we are never outside or spectators to anything in heaven and earth. God doesn't work impersonally from space; He works with us where we are, as He finds us. No matter what we do, whether good or bad, we continue to be a part of everything that God is doing. No one can drop out —there's no place to drop out to. So, we may as well get started and take our place in the story - at the beginning."[1]

CHAPTER 1

HIS MAJESTY'S GPS

The acronym GPS is an abbreviation "for global positioning system and is defined as a system that can show the exact position of a person or thing by using signals from satellites (= objects in space that send signals to earth). Within the context of this system lies varied aspects of models' instruments which provide specific data key to finding one's destination. For example, the GPS tool entitled HERE offers a true representation of what is available in the physical world, presenting POIs (points of interest) that are accurate and deliver meaningful, value-added information."[2] It is said to function in three distinct ways: search and discover, information and interaction.

Much like a GPS system, the Kingdom of Heaven has a divine, supernatural satellite system operated by the King of the Universe, God, Himself. From the beginning of mankind, God bequeathed instruction, direction, disciplines and guidelines to secure a lucrative, fruitful and prosperous transmission of life's signals from the portals of heaven. With so many diverse signals through the atmosphere on the horizon before us, we were designed with supernatural antennas possessing individualized receptors. In order to receive with clear transmission, we have been equipped with the necessary spiritual, physical and emotional mechanisms that allow us to search for and discover constructive information. Being the loving, omnipotent Father, He fashioned us to be empowered for the original intent of effectively, effectually and adequately interacting with all His creation.

Genesis is the premier, noted and preeminent example of this concept. God has always supremely led, guided and directed mankind in a direction for divine purpose, even when their conscious mind was unaware of the subtle prompting. Each chapter in the book of Genesis signifies, depicts or symbolizes guidelines and plans for purpose to be fulfilled.

Beginning in chapter one, of the Bible, entitled the "Creation of the World" (ESV version), all of creation was given notification to assemble in their rightful place. These imperial, magnificent, stately elements of light, water, atmosphere, vegetation and creatures were entirely designed to accommodate the next heavenly satellite signal being transmitted in chapter two. As we arrive on the scene in chapter two entitled, "The Creation of Man and Woman" (AMP version), we are met with our primary points of interest—namely Adam first and then Eve. A divine couple whose designated, appointed, perfect geographical location was described as the Garden of Eden. In this predestined region, they would discover information and be given instruction at their earthly outpost to be fruitful, multiply and have dominion. These lofty, monumental and crucial instructions were particularly devised with the original intent to accomplish, implement, execute and achieve the divine mandate for rulership of the earth realm with customized coordinates from heaven.

By the time we arrive at chapter three in the Bible, "The Fall of Man" (AMP version), we are introduced to our first injunction. Adam and Eve were evicted, banned and forbidden to reside in the Garden of Eden due to a faulty signal being sent from an unauthorized source in addition to an act of Adam's disobedience to follow the original signal and coordinates articulated by God. Like Adam and Eve, many times, we hear the Kingdom mandates, decrees, edits and supernatural, celestial signals from heaven springing forth as the voice of the Lord and/or the Word speaking to our hearts and penetrating our souls. Even though we are brilliantly born with a God-image and God-likeness GPS, we sometimes falter in our failure to hear accurately. Although we are endowed with the power of innovative thought and ingenious reasoning (to identify who we are and our definitive destination), frequently we lack the fortitude, courage or perseverance to obey the signal.

Throughout life's memorable journey comprised of cultural norms, controversial political unrest, radical institutionalized structures, assumptions, attitudes and presumptions, we lose focus and become inundated with earthly influences. These 'signals' of distraction, deception, fear, lies, pride, arrogance and disobedience invade our GPS. We suddenly lose our original signal to be fruitful, multiply and have dominion.

The beauty of the love and grace of Omnipotent God is His navigational system of choice. Choice affords us the privilege and opportunity to cancel any misdirected route or choose a more strategic route that would impact our lives as well as the lives of others. This precise moment of choice is the determining factor where we are assessing our paths, journey and eventually our destination. It is here (like the "HERE" statement from GPS) that we receive Directions for a Divine Destiny.

The direction for a divine destiny is uniquely encrypted in a genetic code. DNA was formulated before the foundation of the world and strategically planted in the embryonic stage of our mother's womb. The journey from birth to life, and from living to dying, are equipped with coordinates which include personalities, peculiarities, assignments, life prescriptions and indicators summoning the signals to announce your arrival—perfect YOU. The YOU—possessing the option of divine timing to activate an appointed journey. The YOU—who's right (correct/obedient) turn will propel you into peaceful, prosperous and productive arrival. Or is it the YOU—who's left (incorrect/disobedient) turn will catapult you into tragic, traumatic and turbulent conditions? The YOU who's unexpected hardship detours steered you through the tunnel of triumph. Following the delegated signal despite the fear and doubt you recognized that coming through also meant—coming out. The YOU who's faith was the compelling compass of conviction with the irrefutable proof that your divine destiny has been established exclusively for you.

Each chapter distinctly sketches a portrait of life permeated with methodologies, intuitive ideologies, innate characteristics and instinctive, emotional passions of a people. From generation to generation, humanity's journey is comprised of cultural distinction, class systems, biased reasoning, intense oppression, struggle for power, social norms, functional and dysfunctional relationships all seeking the satellite signal echoing a resounding voice through time eliciting supreme direction. Now, it is essential that mankind with unwavering faith, intentionally and consistently follow the divine directions constructed to define the purpose, people and places vital to the assignment, commission and sphere of influence for their life's journey. These directions require:

- mapping/coordinates (information)
- updates, re-route, or cancel (life's adjustments)
- precision (careful attention)
- clear vision (competent communication)
- calm atmosphere (proper character)
- identification of destination (knowledge)

GPS directions are like the human characteristic of life which matures and shifts through the navigation of systematic life changes. In some instances, the names of people have been dramatically changed to indicate the transformation of character. Like the GPS system, our directions and vision must be updated and clarified to promote our present future endeavors, to enlarge our mental capacity, to apprehend proper, spiritual guidance and procure the appropriate signal for this divine destiny.

Hearken to the signal from the heavenly satellite!

Adhere to the direction downloaded to earth!

CHAPTER 2

Genesis: Exquisite Perfection

Genesis: a seven day journey, preparing the stage for the greatest event in all of human history—us—Man. The Master Author has flawlessly written the divine quintessential script of all time from the inception to the final act of eternity. Infinite acts too amazing to be numbered and too perfect to be defined—yet each with a Defining Moment.

The supreme, invincible, Almighty, reigning God of the Universe declared it and it was so. Each download into the earth realm blossomed immediately as a visible manifestation of all living creatures and dynamic explosions of creation. Words of power, authority and dominion echoed into the atmosphere with the sound reverberating at the speed of 1,087 feet per second at sea level (before the existence of the salty seas). Words that summoned all creation to exemplary arrangements and the splendid alignments of purpose, intention and design. Creation conceived with expected and ordained ends which could only be altered, changed and rearranged by the Universal Orator, Himself. This magnificent, glorious King of the Universal who originated language, speech, dialogue and dialects spoke—FIRST—existence, life and living into infinity. He spoke all our tomorrows, yesterdays and today. With the jubilant voice of triumphant, these supernatural, invincible words of empowerment from the Omnipotent, Omniscient and Omnipresent God resounded across the abyss and an inevitable destiny of all mankind manifested —IN time and ON time.

His Majesty's Heavenly GPS

> Creation and creatures applaud you, God;
> your holy people bless you.

Psalms 145:10

Genesis: at its very core was heard "The Voice," producing the original, articulate sounds spoken and graciously presented by the Master Orator, on the first day. This divine presentation heralded 5,000–7,000 languages (exclusive of dialects).

Communication—a supreme gift especially tailored for mankind, exploded in the atmosphere. It was the perfect design for a fruitful, beneficial and nourishing relationship of visual and auditory distinction to blossom. Now, humanity would be afforded the opportunity to connect and commune as no other creatures.

Language has been defined as a system of communication that enables humans to exchange verbal and symbolic utterances. Like the Maker who had aligned and positioned all aspects of the creatures, He, of course, must set the protocol by speaking first. In the pre-ordained moment, language cascaded forth from the Master Orator and man chose the identical pattern to proceed into the systematic, organized communication. God was the prototype of the spoken word, thus mankind copied the template of one earthly language and modeled the example for generations to come. (Even then the 1st Amendment rights had been established.) However, after the Babylonian experience, the King of All Creation released a multitude of decrees through spoken languages. Even on that day, God knew that the most prevalent language would be Mandarin Chinese, spoken by 1,213,000,000 people. Those whose parents spoke French would also speak French. Duplication was encrypted in man's DNA by the Maker, symbolizing that all mankind would be like Him, created in His image. He spoke. We speak.

God genetically encoded that which He designed to be necessary for the genius of thought and expression, both grammatical and semantic categories. As man was empowered by this distinguished,

Genesis: Exquisite Perfection

renowned form of communication, fashioned in audible (modality), sign language (visual) and Braille (tactile), these noble human beings acquired intellect pursuits of reasoning, understanding, thought, judgment, brain power and wisdom. This resulted in cultivating refined social interaction and effective decision-making on "Day One" when—He spoke.

God's supreme, glorious and celestial words, which scripted the lyric of the songbird and the crooning of a newborn baby, or the rambunctious roar of the lion in the daring depth of the jungle, constructed all of eternity. Words fashioned the daylight and draped the darkness of the night; words provoked the flash of lightning and the intense rumbling of the oceanic waters as He commanded it to obey its boundaries. Penetrating, profound, powerful words which demanded a parting of waters identified as the Red Sea measuring 190 miles across, 1,200 miles long, maximum depth of 8,200 feet and average depth of 1,640 feet and hurled its furious waves, erecting stately walls and exposing a sandy surface of dry land. Oceanography took its first bow to the Creator King.

With no audience present to applaud this momentous occasion, this holy, spoken sound emanated out of space and into space setting a precedence of obedience for which all the earth would surrender. This would be a "call" so intense, so fierce, that over a hundred mountains of the Himalayas with its highest peak on the planet would have no recourse but to heed the call (including Mount Everest), be erected, fashioned, and formed by this divine protocol and never, ever depart from their proclaimed positions.

Agriculture pranced on the scene. Trees would emerge rooted in the dark hues of an earthy soil, flowing with stems and branches, rich, green leaves, poised to change with the entrance of the four seasons, and sumptuous, delectable fruit—at the proclamation of the Almighty, Invincible, Immutable God. Trees whose lifespan stretched for thousands of years brought into existence by the breath and word of a miraculous horticulturist called God. The God who sprinkled the seed across the fertile grounds He created and sprouted forth just over three trillion fully grown trees in the earth realm. From the Cypress of Abarkuh located in Abakuh, Yazd Province, Iran and estimated to be 4,500 years old and the second oldest living tree in the world to the "Cedar of God" located in the northern mountains of Lebanon, also known as the cedars of Lebanon, which is a symbol of the Messiah, seen in the Bible over seventy times, all divinely designed, birthed and sustained by its Master Creator. Similar in profoundness is the survival of 170 Hibakujumoku trees located in Hiroshima, Japan, during the atomic bombing of Hiroshima while others withered and died. But the Master has orchestrated the course of their existence, even the trees, like the expiration date of all creation. Oh, the magnificence!

> "God is not only an omnipotent Creator, not just a brilliant strategist or a Mighty Captain, but a loving Shepherd who leads and guides His people with a rod and staff."
>
> John Maxwell
> *The Maxwell Leadership Bible*, Introduction to Psalms[3]

Royal Decree

This is the history of [the origin of] the heavens and of the earth when they were created, in the day [that is, days of creation] that the LORD God made the earth and the heavens.

Genesis 2:4 (AMP)

At the beginning You founded the earth; the heavens are the work of Your hands.

Psalms 102:25 (AMP)

This is the book (the written record, the history) of the generations of [the descendants of] Adam. When God created man, He made him in the likeness of God [not physical, but a spiritual personality and moral likeness].

Genesis 5:1 (AMP)

His Majesty's Heavenly GPS

ROYAL MELODY

I SING THE MIGHTY POWER OF GOD

I sing the mighty power of God that made the mountain rise,
That spread the flowing seas abroad and built the lofty skies,
I sing the wisdom that ordained the sun to rule the day;
The moon shines full at His command, and all the stars obey.

I sing the goodness of the Lord that filled the earth with food;
He formed creatures with His Word and then pronounced them good,
Lord, how Your wonders are displayed where'er I turn my eye,
If I survey the ground I tread or gaze upon the sky!

There's not a plant or flower below but makes your glories known;
And clouds arise and tempests blow by order from Your throne;
While all that borrow life from You is ever in Your care,
And everywhere that I may be, You, God are present there.

English Hymnist, Isaac Watts, 1715

CHAPTER 3

Genesis: The Beginning

Genesis, the Original, that which is present or existing from the beginning (first or earliest). The Original—created directly and personally by a particular artist, not a copy or imitation. Sovereign God, Author of the Universe, Author of the Beginning. had a set time, a defining moment, when purpose and protocol took its place. There was this awesome, phenomenal place where the Earth heard the sound of the Master's call and responded. In the midst of nothingness, time interrupted eternity as the Commander-in-Chief gave the orders. The command was heard and obedience was birthed. It was birthed as a command that stood at attention and carefully carried out every distinct, authoritative order.

Genesis, where the colors of the rainbow leaped onto the surface of the earth, stroking an enormous, blue sky as it awaited the entrance of the rain to displace its grandiose designed drops. Genesis, where flamboyant floral emerged in the midst of the plush blanket of green grass sprinkled with shades of lavender wisteria petals, stroked by the hand of the Master, while the ravishing red of a rose petal cascaded in a perfect array of elegant glory. The Artist of all time splashed a hint of aqua, teal and turquoise into the ocean deep as it swirled through the rivers, streams and seashores for all times, never leaving its set boundaries.

Genesis, where the celestial sky captivated its first electrical system. Stars of ten billion different volts twinkled on command, lighting the universe with an impressive display of divine illumination. This light-emitting diode (LED) formation was flicked

His Majesty's Heavenly GPS

on by the Sovereign King of the Universe and staged perfectly in the regal atmosphere of the majestic moonlight. Then the Great, Omniscient God, Elohay Kedem (God of the Beginning), timed the birth of Oleg Vladimirovich Losev, a Russian scientist and inventor, who lacked a formal education and released through him the first light-emitting diode (LED) in 1927.

Continuing in His glorious champion of men, God divinely selected James R. "Bob" Biard, an American electrical engineer and inventor, to further expand His original plan as it related to illumination and light. In October 1962, Biard and his colleague, Gary Pittman, proclaimed the first commercial light-emitting diode (LED) product, the SNX-100. Just as the Master had planned it, this SNX-100 produced a 900 nm light output from the contents of a pure gallium arsenide (GaAs) crystal. Little did Biard know that he had been chosen before May 20, 1931, his birth date, to participate with the Almighty God in the industrial enhancement of mankind.

During the same time span of 1962, God commissioned an inventor and 2008 inductee into the National Inventors Hall of Fame, Nick Holonyak Jr., to invent another form of the light-emitting diode (LED). This time, Holonyak with his brilliant, God-given mind, under divine inspiration, captured the LED that emitted visible, red light instead of infrared light. How awesome is our God with his continuous gifting of methods, means and ways to build and sustain His more perfect way. Holonyak went on to acquire 41 patents which included various, innovative designs that launched us forward into the technological age with CD players, DVD players and cell phones that use the laser diode, as well as an apparatus used in light dimmers and power tools called the "p-n-p-n" switch. Still expanding, increasing and extending His master plan through eternity, His purpose is fulfilled for our good and His glory. Where would we be today if this part of the plan had not been obeyed by Holonyak from the voice of the Creator? We can reflect upon and ponder the truth of our loving Father God who

Genesis: The Beginning

never ceases to advance the channels through which our comfort, convenience and care remain paramount for all He has established from the inauguration of creation.

Losev, Biard and Holonyak were just a few identified among the thousands who trail blazed the multi-faceted realm of light and illumination beginning on the first day and trickled and rippled down through phases and stages of life. Without a conscious thought of their uniqueness, divine appointments or delegated authority, God certified them from the heavenlies. They may or may not have realized that their inspiration came from Him. However, they accepted the nomination and we became benefactors of the yielding obedience to the boundless extension of that first day. In His sovereign will and foreknowledge, God presented them with the monumental task of further defining, describing and interpreting those things which He alone designed in His original blueprint.

Genesis, when and where the voice of the Creator instructed the switch of eternity to turn on its power of about 386 billion billion megawatts from the center of this solar system. This incomparable energy source (a giant star) is called the sun. (I call this star Sir Sun.) This magnificent, spectacular, brilliant light, ruling the earth by day, is too hot to handle by any living creature. It sizzles at 5,778 Kelvins and is too far to take a stroll on a sunny afternoon, at a distance of 92.96 million miles from earth. Gloriously, it made its entrance on the galactic scene. In the splendor of that fourth day, the exclusive Mastermind of the universe, God Himself, echoed into existence an endless number of perpetual, relentless lights, for illumination across the parameters of this great universe. No man would be given designated authority to this celestial "power switch." The Most High God and King of the Universe would have supreme dominance over this astronomical source of power and energy.

Sir Sun, heaven's alarm clock, with its impeccable timing and matchless brightness, speaks expressly to the dawning of a new

His Majesty's Heavenly GPS

day and softly to the entrance of night. This flawless, superlative combination of exact measures of constructed chemical components broadcast its splendor from dawn to dusk.

A.J. Lawless, an acclaimed poet, once wrote:

> "It was sunsets that taught me that beauty sometimes
> Only last for a couple of moments,
> And it was sunrises that showed me that all it takes
> Is patience to experience it all over again."[4]

Lawless listened and learned from the first day's endowment to express her awareness of beauty and patience.

Amidst this miraculous, supernatural creation, day five was reserved for the partnership of aeronautics and aviation. Genesis, when the wandering albatross, with a wingspan of 8 feet 3 inches to 11 feet 6 inches was created, known to fly the southern ocean in one year (covering more than 75,000 miles). The bald eagle's speed of 75-99 miles per hour also gave rise to the beauty and intrigue of aerodynamics. Little did Orville and Wilbur Wright know that they had been chosen and ordained to upgrade His original creation and customize it to the fabric of men with divine purpose and of vital necessity in its generation and beyond. From the first flight of wondrous, winged creatures to the architectural design of the Boeing 777 airplane, the Magnificent Maker of heaven and earth crafted them all, either directly or indirectly.

Royal Decree

Do what GOD tells you.
Walk in the paths He shows you:
Follow the life-map absolutely,
Keep an eye out for the signposts,
His course for life set out
In the revelation to Moses;
Then you'll get on well
In whatever you do and wherever you go.

1 Kings 2:3

The revelation of GOD is whole
and pulls our lives together.
The signposts of GOD are clear
and point out the right road.
The life-maps of GOD are right,
showing the way to joy.
The directions of GOD are plain
and easy on the eyes.
GOD's reputation is twenty-four-carat gold,
with a lifetime guarantee.
The decisions of GOD are accurate
down to the nth degree.

Psalms 19:7-9

CHAPTER 4

GENESIS: THE POWER OF FIRST

"First" is defined as:

- preceding all others of a series or kind
- the ordinal of one
- earliest
- most eminent or exalted; most excellent, chief, highest
- before anything else
- the person or thing in the first position
- something that has NEVER happened before; a new occurrence
- primary
- preceding all others in time, order or importance; such as earliest
- for the first time
- in preference to something else
- first occurrence or item of a kind
- at the beginning (initially)
- coming before all others in time, order or importance

The essence of beginning and first is that it is incomparable. Forever, it is a template created from the original creation.

Bless God, all creatures, wherever you are—
everything and everyone made by God.
Psalms 103:21

His Majesty's Heavenly GPS

Creation can be defined as a seven day journey for all of human history to be etched out and time-released by the Master Creator for generations, eras and ages to come. Each physiological and biological substance or inventor unconsciously awaits the entrance and purpose of a definitive, divine manifestation for the progression of life. Manifestations yet unknown, whose characters and natures have been perfectly preordained and designed. Now, creation springs forth on its specified "due date." Due dates which we refer to as "birth dates."

We have come to understand that the birth date, whether creation, creature or invention, is expressed by man to fulfill a divine purpose with clarity of intent and performance of perfection as it relates to its identity. For example, as we subliminally enjoy the pleasure, peace and contentment of knowing that the boundaries of the waters have been given command to only sweep the edges of the seashore with limited range, we bask on the sandy shores of our beaches. We stand secure, without thought, that the overflow of a riverbank on a normal day will not drown us. Here, the waters have obeyed their first command and they will continue for eternity in that obedience for the amusement and safety of all mankind.

The first command sounded by our loving Father God to the sun contained the unheard determination announcing that the blazing glow of the sun (with a blistering temperature of 5,505 degrees Celsius and 9,941 degrees Farenheit) will not scorch us on a sweltering, tropical, summer day, unless we violate the law of exposure to sunlight and its many dangers.

This Great God Almighty, Master Creator, has set in place an environment conducive to the flourishing growth of the magnificent creature called "MAN" in His first commands.

Genesis: The Power of First

The sound of our personal, human history reverberates through our minds with sweet, familiar thoughts as we reflect upon the—FIRST. As we reminisce on the profound feeling we felt or the transformation that changed the course of time because there was this—FIRST.

We can remember our—
- First toy
- First day of school excitement
- First public, pleasant recognition at school
- First time winning an important game of championship
- First time getting and riding our bicycles
- First love
- First boyfriend/girlfriend
- First date
- First kiss
- First hurt
- First time driving a car
- First car
- First job

just to name a few.

Each time there is a thought of any of these things, there is a mental trigger that releases special moments (landmarks) that lead to the next dimension of our lives. There is a recognition that something of paramount proportions has slipped into our lives and altered it forever. It has the capacity to change our thinking, realign our relationships, and reposition our destinies as we discover that no matter how wonderful and beautiful our first impression of man might have been, there is a deeper measure we will experience in the process of time.

These days, as we experience this fast, technological growth, pace and sometimes turbulent times, there are those moments when we can barely remember how and where it all began. Our recollection of the old has faded into the new. We stand in awe of what we now see and wonder what will be our next "first" to impact human history. What could be the next FIRST that would change the world as we now perceive it?

What must have gone on in the minds of Adam and Eve when they felt that clothing had become a necessity? Clothing was a concept which previously had no relevance to their lifestyle. Imagine their reaction as they held their first newborn, male child (another human being, first vaginal birth through the womb of Eve and the seed of Adam).

Then we remember that the Omniscient Sovereign Lord God is Alpha and Omega, the First and the Last. He is the Omnipotent God, Master of the universe, in whom we place our trust. We understand that His ways are perfect and there are no surprises to Him. The Creator and Author has set every FIRST and aligned it according to His purpose, through our potential and His divinely orchestrated, extraordinary plan.

Genesis: The Power of First

First Mentions & Scriptures

- Act of Order: Creation: Heaven and Earth (Genesis 1:1)
- Light (Genesis 1:3)
- Day (Genesis 1:5)
- Night (Genesis 1:5)
- Sky and Water (Genesis 1:6)
- Sprinkler System (Genesis 1:6)
- Land and Water (Genesis 1:10)
- Seed-Bearing Plant/Fruit: Reproduction (Genesis 1:11-13)
- Seasons, Sun, Moon (Genesis 1:14-19)
- Command/Order - God to Man (Genesis 1:16)
- Ichthyology – Fish; Ornithology - Birds (Genesis 1:20-23)
- Animals (Genesis 1:24-25)
- Man's Dominion Over the Earth (Genesis 1:26, 28-31)
- Rest Declared (Genesis 2:1-3)
- Man Created: Adam, First Breath (Genesis 2:7)
- Residence: Garden of Eden (Genesis 2:8)
- Community - Eden (Genesis 2:8)
- Agriculture (Genesis 2:8)
- Good and Evil (Genesis 2:9)
- Gold (Genesis 2:11)
- Named River - Pishon (Genesis 2:11)
- Named Goldmine - Havilah (Genesis 2:11)
- Farmer: Adam (Genesis 2:15)
- Instruction Given to Man (Genesis 2:16-17)
- Educational System (Genesis 2:19)
- Biologist: Adam (Genesis 2:19-20)
- Surgeon: God (Genesis 2:21-22)
- Female: Eve (Genesis 2:22-23)

His Majesty's Heavenly GPS

- Marital Covenant (Genesis 2:24)
- Con Artist: Serpent (Genesis 3:1)
- The Lie (Genesis 3:4)
- Deception (Genesis 3:6, 13)
- Tailors/Creativity - Fig Leaves for Clothing (Genesis 3:7)
- Question - God Asked Adam (Genesis 3:9)
- First Curse - God Cursed the Serpent (Genesis 3:14)
- Physical Pain - Pregnancy/Childbirth (Genesis 3:16)
- Curse Pronounced on Man (Genesis 3:17-19)
- Employment (Genesis 3:17)
- Mother (Genesis 3:20)
- Name Chosen by Man - Adam Named Eve (Genesis 3:20)
- Fashion Designer - God (Genesis 3:21)
- Dispossession, Eviction (Genesis 3:23-24)
- Security Guards - Cheribum of the Most High God (Genesis 3:24)
- Human Conception/Childbirth: Cain (Genesis 4:1)
- Sibling - Abel (Genesis 4:2)
- First Called Shepherd - Abel (Genesis 4:2)
- First Called Farmer - Cain (Genesis 4:2)
- Offering - Cain Fruit of the Ground (Genesis 4:3)
- Animal's Birth - Abel's First-Born Flock (Genesis 4:4)
- Sibling Rivalry (Genesis 4:4-5)
- Emotion - Jealousy (Genesis 4:5)
- Psychotic Outburst/Temper Tantrum - Cain (Genesis 4:5-6)
- Murder - Cain Killed Abel (Genesis 4:8)
- First Mention of Bloodshed - Blood Speaks (Genesis 4:10)
- Curse Pronounced (Genesis 4:11)
- Homeless - Cain (Genesis 4:12)
- Fugitive - Cain (Genesis 4:14)
- Tattoo - Cain Marked for Protection (Genesis 4:15)

Genesis: The Power of First

- Term "Wife" (Genesis 4:17)
- Grandchild: Enoch (Genesis 4:17)
- First Real Estate Developer - Cain (Genesis 4:17)
- Great-Grandson - Irad (Genesis 4:18)
- Physical Marriage Covenant - Lamech and Adah, and Lamech and Zillah (Genesis 4:19)
- Cowboy/Cattleman: Jabal (Genesis 4:20)
- Musician - Inventor of Harp & Flute - Jubal (Genesis 4:21)
- Teacher and Craftsman: Tubal-Cain (Genesis 4:22)
- Construction - Metal Worker - Tubal-Cain (Genesis 4:22)
- Recorded Female Birth - Sister - Naamah (Genesis 4:22)
- Replacement Child - Seth (Genesis 4:25)
- Worship to Almighty God (Genesis 4:26)
- Man, First Called Adam (Mankind, Human) (Genesis 5:2)
- Supernatural Ascension: Enoch (Genesis 5:24)
- Giants (Genesis 6:4)
- Favor Spoken Concerning Noah (Genesis 6:8)
- Boat (Genesis 6:14)
- First Architect and Engineer - Noah (Genesis 6:14)
- First Sailor - Noah (Genesis 6:22)
- First Shipmates - Shem, Ham, Japheth (Genesis 7:1)
- Rain (Genesis 7:4)
- Introduction of Months (Genesis 7:11)
- First Shut-In (Genesis 7:16)
- Tsunami (Genesis 7:20-22)
- Human Annihilation (Genesis 7:22-23)
- Grace - Noah Remains Alive (Genesis 7:23)
- Altar/Offering (Genesis 8:20)
- Pronounced Blessing (Genesis 9:1)
- Dietary (Genesis 9:3)
- Covenant Promise - Rainbow (Genesis 9:12-13)

His Majesty's Heavenly GPS

- Wine (Genesis 9:20-21)
- Substance Abuse - Drunk - Noah (Genesis 9:21)
- Indecent Exposure - Noah (Genesis 9:22)
- Servant - Canaanites (Genesis 9:25-26)
- Empire (Genesis 10:8-12)
- Skyscraper (Genesis 11:4-5)
- Multiple Languages (Genesis 11:7)
- Ethnicity Developed (Genesis 11:8)
- Child's Death Before the Parent (Genesis 11:28)
- Barrenness - Sarah (Genesis 11:30)
- Immigrant - Abraham (Genesis 12:1)
- Millionaire - Abraham (Genesis 13:2)
- Kings (Genesis 14:1)
- Priest: Melchizedek (Genesis 14:18)
- Tithes (Genesis 14:20)
- Person Named Before Birth - Ishmael (Genesis 16:11)
- Incest - Lot's Daughter (Genesis 19:31-38)

CHAPTER 5

GENESIS: THE MARVEL OF MAN

"Man represents the highest order of creation
and the greatest masterpiece of God's artistry."
Myles Munroe, *The Glory Living*[5]

I thank you, High God—you're breathtaking!
Body and soul, I am marvelously made!
I worship in adoration—what a creation!
You know me inside and out,
you know every bone in my body;
You know exactly how I was made, bit by bit,
how I was sculpted from nothing into something.
Like an open book, you watched me grow from conception
to birth; all the stages of my life were spread out before you,
The days of my life all prepared before I'd even lived.

Psalms 139:13-16

Day six, the anticipation of the earth to receive the greatest miracle of all creation—Man. Man, whom God so meticulously and perfectly designed, fashioned and constructed from His divine, luxurious, celestial dust. This man, appropriately called Adam, was an exquisite, artistic, miraculous design that was immaculately poised and suited for the dust from which he was formed. Adam, the most glorious of all the Master has created, was strategically positioned to receive this "breath of life." From the beginning, until this present time, a man is considered to be alive if he is *breathing*.

His Majesty's Heavenly GPS

The transference of this one sacred, anointed breath from the Holy, Divine Creator impregnated Adam with the image of the Maker producing nationalities, creeds, and ethnicities, with varied cultures and specified civilizations. Multiplication took on a new meaning with this one breath. Distinctions, diversities and differences sat at the head of the table of life dictating commands and orders which summoned creativity, originality and productivity as its VIP guests. Civilizations escorted by social classes, ideologies, and revolutions were invited as well. Having an affinity for enlightenment, civilization bonded with thought and expression while imagination enticed realization.

After the seventh day, as God gave residency to Adam in Eden, God downloaded the regal, mental capacity of genius into the mind of Adam. He was now responsible for identifying the biological classification and taxonomic rank of every living creation. Prompted by his divine nature, Adam did not hesitate to classify an estimated 5-30 million organisms in his world. Even though, according to God's timing many years later (1737), the Swedish botanist, Carl Linnaeus, was regarded as the "Father of Taxonomy." Truly, Adam was the original taxonomist as he announced that which he heard from the Divine Botanist. This unique and profound relationship caused the download to echo from the Mind of God to the mind of Adam to express God's supernatural nature.

The essence of arrangement and order had begun and through-out time, generation after generation, God extracted from mankind that which He had purposed the very day He spoke. Like the ripple of the waves of time, His original mandate keeps speaking—in His divine order, His perfect will, with precise purpose and exact protocol.

Genesis, the time before time. The place where *Chronos* and *Kairos* kissed each other, awaiting the divine timing set by the

Sovereign God to release what had already been spoken—"In the beginning." (*Chronos* and *Kairos* are Greek words translated "time" which have subtle differences in meaning. *Chronos* means a specific division of time—like a day, hour, minute, etc.—while *kairos* means a specific moment or season often appointed by God.)

With all acts of Himself being displayed—power, dominion and authority—the Originator of the Source of Life has declared, decreed, proclaimed and established it ALL AT ONCE! Every generation, destination and socialization has been established. Once and for all, "In the Beginning": GENESIS.

So I give you.......GENESIS.

CHAPTER 6

GENESIS: THE MEANING

The Book of Genesis is the revelation of the Elohistic (Creative) power of an Omniscient, Omnipresent and Omnipotent God: the only, true and living God. Everything in the universe was created by Him – God alone. God created everything with a plan, on purpose, through a progression of time.

When we submit to the awesome, creative Holy Spirit of our God and align ourselves with His will, we also create greatness for His honor and glory to prove what is that good and perfect gift in Christ Jesus. For we are truly created in His image and after His likeness.

Come! Join me, as we follow the Word of God on this journey of revelation and power for living.

> The very steps we take come from God;
> otherwise how would we
> know where we are going?
>
> **Proverbs 20:24**

His Majesty's Heavenly GPS

ROYAL DECREE
THE WORD, THE WORK

THE HEAVENS PROCLAIM THE GLORY OF GOD.
THE SKIES DISPLAY HIS CRAFTSMANSHIP.
DAY AFTER DAY THEY CONTINUE TO SPEAK;
NIGHT AFTER NIGHT THEY MAKE HIM KNOWN.
THEY SPEAK WITHOUT A SOUND OR WORD;
THEIR VOICE IS NEVER HEARD.
YET THEIR MESSAGE HAS GONE THROUGHOUT THE EARTH,
AND THEIR WORDS TO ALL THE WORLD.

PSALMS 19:1-4 (NLT)

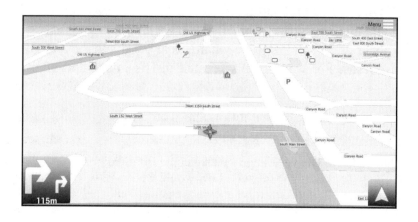

I'M WRITING OUT CLEAR DIRECTIONS TO WISDOM WAY,
I'M DRAWING A MAP TO RIGHTEOUS ROAD.

PROVERBS 4:11

CHAPTER 7

THE HEAVENLY GPS

I find it so astounding that in this time of human history, our Sovereign God would, once again, create through the minds of men a distinct, unique, and uncommon way in which to describe and interpret by use of more specific, precise, explicit ways of finding our direction. Could it be that in this present season, we are searching deeper than ever, the magnitude concerning the supernatural, mysterious, intricate, incomprehensible, unfathomable enigma of "Creation." To suggest that there was necessity to design an instrument perfectly named MapQuest would imply that the journey is limitless as it relates to time, thought and perception of where we are going or where others have been.

A "journey" is defined as something suggesting travel or passage from one place to another; the journey from youth to maturity; a journey through time. So, we ponder this seven-day journey at the beginning impregnated with ALL of time. Here, we find ourselves traveling through—a definitive time (better known as our generation) in history that set the protocol for ALL of time. A time before us and after us has been proclaimed in these seven days, when only the God of the Universe has written the final chapter and established the comings and goings of each era and each generation. Where will we find ourselves? How will we know when to navigate to the next place of potential or possibility? Who will be on our journey? What will we encounter along the way? How long will the journey be? Who will go with us? Who will we meet and why?

His Majesty's Heavenly GPS

This magnificent tool described as MapQuest (originally established as Cartographic Services) reminds us of our personal journeys. It was conceived as a United States, free, online mapping service owned by Verizon. God, once again, had divinely chosen world changers and thought leaders with intentional, technological geniuses beginning in 1967 known as R.R. Donnelley & Sons in Chicago, whose original idea first began from a cartographic company. Later, they were joined by the executive team of Barry Glick, Perry Evans, Simon Greenman, Edward Mance and Harry Grout. However, like great men who had gone before them, they were elected and selected to be on their journeys, as they perfected and clarified the physical maps and route navigation for others. Once again, whether they were consciously in a relationship with the Creator or not, they were used by Him to transmit a new level of intelligence which can be used by all people for righteous purposes.

And so, as God has purposed, positioned and aligned each creature and act of creation in a time zone in an ever-evolving world, we set our hearts and spirits to navigate our lives to discover the path that is prepared before us; our minds to adequately, competently and efficiently chart the course with wisdom, knowledge and understanding. Like the evolution and process of MapQuest, of its name evolving over time (it was not until 1999 that the company was renamed to MapQuest). In 2000, so has the journey of mankind evolved, changed, transformed and reformed over time.

As I began to chronicle the Book of Genesis, even in the first two chapters, I realized the analogy that the Master had downloaded into my mind, was so tremendous and succint in depicting, characterizing, and illuminating how our life journey is so perfectly etched out throughout each family, generation, culture and time. Like the MapQuest, an online mapping application, we are perpetually, continuously navigating our "on-life" application with a strategic mapping application that believers call the Bible. Like MapQuest, who compete with other competitors of high value in the field, (it is

The Heavenly GPS

still the top performer) so is the Bible. With estimated sales of over five billion copies, it is widely considered to be the most influential and best-selling book of all time. Similarities, too many to mention align themselves within our life journey, such as:

- MapQuest uses some of TomTom's services for its mapping system.

- MapQuest provides some extent of street-level detail and/or driving directions for a variety of countries.

- MapQuest offers a free mobile app for Android and iOS that features Point of Interest (POI) search, voice-guided navigation, real-time traffic and other features. MapQuest also offers a mobile-friendly website.

- MapQuest Discover is a site for finding interesting travel destinations, and Travel Blogs is a tool with which users can publish photos and blog entries about their vacations and travel.

- MapQuest's Points of Interest (POI) data helps the service differentiate itself from other wayfinding software by guiding users directly to the entrances of businesses and destinations, rather than to general street addresses." In cases where we have arrived at a temporary destination of discomfort, crisis, unexpected, unprepared promotion, disappointment or ignorance concerning where we are, there is a necessity of a tour guide.

A tour guide or a tourist guide is a person who aids or gives information on cultural, historical and contemporary heritage on organized tours and to individual clients at educational establishments, religious and historical sites, museums, and at venues of other significance. According to the Word of God, God has supplied us with a tour guide described as the Holy Spirit; some have referred to Him as mere intuition or prophetic insight. However, it goes deeper—for within the seven days of creation, provision was made for us to gain spiritual, psychological, and gifted assistance to navigate the residence of our culture, documentation of our historical foundations, organized through symbols, pictures and archives of unprecedented, constructed monuments, buildings and even caves. These subordinate tour guides have strategic roles assigned according to the situation of the tour. The language is comprehensive to the viewer. Guides represent and are qualified to interpret the culture and heritage mundane to the heritage of a people (and so it is with Spirit-inspired Scripture). Because of the crucial, significant, essential responsibility of the heaven-sent Tour Guide, it is vitally important that we cooperate with the strong communication skills, punctuality and keen sense of direction characterized as paramount qualities He possesses.

So now, we will set our GPS and set the navigation to begin at the beginning – Genesis. This has accurately been laid out for all on this part of the journey. Like our Creator, the MapQuest did not wait for everyone to request where to go. He had already designed where they should go with a plan and purpose. He now only waited for each one to communicate with His omniscient power and receive the divine, ordained, earth assignment that would perpetually change all human history from era to era as He had finished the end at the beginning.

A "map" is defined as a symbolic depiction emphasizing the relationship between elements of some space, such as objects, regions or themes. We chose the theme of life's creation.

As we coordinate the main functions of maps, we create a location map based upon our address, city, zip code, purpose, assignment, potential, capacity, skill, talent, ability and calling. The view from Kingdom perspective will give insight to our own magnificent journeys. We will not forget to review the Driving Directions, which generate a route from "Point A" to "Point B" based on as

much address information as you can provide (Scripture) and it will estimate how long it will take you to get there. What vision have you pursued? What goals have you set to get there? What is navigating your direction? Is it fear or faith? What traffic of negativity must be avoided to reach your destination the exact time it has been planned by our Creator?

We set our routes and add our stops (scriptures). Even before our OnStar button is set to request, Madam Grace has given us a step-by-step direction of where we are going. Our faith has taught us that we are assured of the revelation, socialization, generational communication and complication patterns that we shall overcome to reach our destination. These issues have been encapsulated within the human experience as it was ordained—in the Beginning.

CHAPTER 8

Prologue to the GPS Coordinates

To receive an even greater understanding of this book, we have provided for you not one, but two tables that show the chapter titles; however, this one is unique because it shows them in the various versions of the Bible.

The first set shows the chapter titles as presented by the English Standard Version (ESV), Amplified Version (AMP), and The Message Bible (MSG). The second set shows the Titles as presented by the New International Version (NIV), New Living Translation (NLT), and the New King James Version (NKJV). As a note, there were no chapter titles for the King James Version (KJV).

Chapter	English Standard Version (ESV)	Amplified Version (AMP)	Message Bible (MSG)
1	The Creation of the World	The Creation	Heaven and Earth
2	The Seventh Day, God Rests	The Creation of Man and Woman	Adam and Eve
3	The Fall	The Fall of Man	
4	Cain and Abel	Cain and Abel	
5	Adam's Descendants to Noah	Descendants of Adam	The Family Tree of the Human Race

His Majesty's Heavenly GPS

Chapter	English Standard Version (ESV)	Amplified Version (AMP)	Message Bible (MSG)
6	Increasing Corruption on Earth	The Corruption of Mankind	Giants in the Land
7		The Flood	
8	The Flood Subsides	The Flood Abates	
9		Covenant of the Rainbow	
10	Nations Descended from Noah	Descendants of Noah	The Family Tree of Noah's Sons
11	The Tower of Babel	Universal Language, Babel, Confusion	God Turned Their Language into Babble
12	The Call of Abram	Abram's Journey to Egypt	Abram and Sarai
13	Abram and Lot Separate	Abram and Lot	
14	Abram Rescues Lot	War of the Kings	

Prologue to the GPS Coordinates

Chapter	English Standard Version (ESV)	Amplified Version (AMP)	Message Bible (MSG)
15	God's Covenant with Abram	Abram Promised a Son	
16	Sarai and Hagar	Sarai and Hagar	
17	Abraham and the Covenant of Circumcision	Abraham and the Covenant of Circumcision	
18		Birth of Isaac Promised	
19	God Rescues Lot	The Doom of Sodom	
20	Abraham and Abimelech	Abraham's Deception	
21	The Birth of Isaac	Isaac Is Born	
22	The Sacrifice of Isaac	The Offering of Isaac	
23	Sarah's Death and Burial	Death and Burial of Sarah	
24	Isaac and Rebekah	A Bride for Isaac	Isaac and Rebekah

His Majesty's Heavenly GPS

Chapter	English Standard Version (ESV)	Amplified Version (AMP)	Message Bible (MSG)
25	Abraham's Death and His Descendants	Abraham's Death	
26	God's Promise to Isaac	Isaac Settles in Gerar	
27	Isaac Blesses Jacob	Joseph's Deception	
28	Jacob Sent to Laban	Jacob Is Sent Away	
29	Jacob Marries Leah and Rachel	Jacob Meets Rachel	
30		The Sons of Jacob	
31	Jacob Flees from Laban	Jacob Leaves Secretly for Canaan	
32	Jacob Fears Esau	Jacob's Fear of Esau	
33	Jacob Meets Esau	Jacob Meets Esau	

Prologue to the GPS Coordinates

Chapter	English Standard Version (ESV)	Amplified Version (AMP)	Message Bible (MSG)
34	The Defiling of Dinah	The Treachery of Jacob's Sons	
35	God Blesses and Renames Jacob	Jacob Moves to Bethel	
36	Esau's Descendants	Esau Moves	
37	Joseph's Dream	Joseph's Dream	Joseph and His Brothers
38	Judah and Tamar	Judah and Tamar	
39	Joseph and Potiphar's Wife	Joseph's Success in Egypt	
40	Joseph Interprets Two Prisoners' Dreams	Joseph Interprets a Dream	
41	Joseph Interprets Pharaoh's Dream	Pharaoh's Dream	

His Majesty's Heavenly GPS

Chapter	English Standard Version (ESV)	Amplified Version (AMP)	Message Bible (MSG)
42	Joseph's Brothers Go to Egypt	Joseph's Brothers Sent to Egypt	
43	Joseph's Brothers Return to Egypt	The Return to Egypt	
44	Joseph Tests His Brothers	The Brothers Are Brought Back	
45	Joseph Provides for His Brothers and Family	Joseph Shows Kindness to His Brothers	
46	Joseph Brings His Family to Egypt	Jacob Moves to Egypt	
47	Jacob's Family Settles in Goshen	Jacob's Family Settles in Goshen	
48	Jacob Blesses Ephraim and Manasseh	Israel's (Jacob) Last Days	
49	Jacob Blesses His Sons	Israel's (Jacob) Prophecy Concerning His Sons	
50		Burial Preparation and Mourning for Jacob	

Prologue to the GPS Coordinates

PROLOGUE CONTINUED OTHER BIBLE VERSIONS

Chapter	New International Version (NIV)	New Living Translation (NLT)	New King James Version (NKJV)
1	The Beginning	The Account of Creation	The Creation
2	Adam and Eve	The Man and Woman in Eden	The Garden of Eden
3	The Fall	The Man and Woman Sin	The Fall of Man
4	Cain and Abel	Cain and Abel	Cain and Abel
5	From Adam to Noah	The Descendants of Adam	The Family of Adam
6	Wickedness in This World	A World Gone Wrong	Noah Makes an Ark
7	Noah and the Flood	The Flood Covers the Earth	The Flood
8		The Flood Recedes	The Flood Waters Recede
9	God's Covenant with Noah	God Confirms His Covenant	God's Promise to Noah

His Majesty's Heavenly GPS

Chapter	New International Version (NIV)	New Living Translation (NLT)	New King James Version (NKJV)
10	The Table of Nations	Descendants of Japheth/Ham	Nations That Descended from Noah
11	The Tower of Babel	The Tower of Babel	The Tower of Babel
12	The Call of Abram	The Call of Abram	God Speaks to Abram
13	Abram and Lot Separate	Abram and Lot Separate	Abram Inherits Canaan
14	Abram Rescues Lot	Abram Rescues Lot	Lot's Capture and Rescue
15	The Lord's Covenant with Abram	The Lord's Covenant Promise to Abram	God's Promise to Abram
16	Hagar and Ishmael	The Birth of Ishmael	Hagar and Ishmael
17	The Covenant of Circumcision	Abram Is Named Abraham	The Sign of God's Promise to Abraham
18	The Three Visitors	A Son Is Promised to Sarah	A Son Is Promised

Prologue to the GPS Coordinates

Chapter	New International Version (NIV)	New Living Translation (NLT)	New King James Version (NKJV)
19	Sodom and Gomorrah Destroyed	Sodom and Gomorrah Destroyed	Two Evil Cities Destroyed
20	Abraham and Abimelech	Abraham Deceives Abimelech	Abraham and Abimelech
21	The Birth of Isaac	The Birth of Isaac	Isaac Is Born
22	Abraham Tested	Abraham's Faith Tested	Abraham Commanded to Offer Isaac
23	Nahor's Sons	The Burial of Sarah	Death and Burial of Sarah
24	Isaac and Rebekah	A Wife for Isaac	Rebekah Chosen as a Wife for Isaac
25	The Death of Abraham	The Death of Abraham	Birth of Esau and Jacob
26	Isaac and Abimelech	Isaac Deceives Abimelech	Isaac and Abimelech
27	Jacob Takes Esau's Blessing	Jacob Steals Esau's Blessing	Jacob Receives Isaac's Blessing

His Majesty's Heavenly GPS

Chapter	New International Version (NIV)	New Living Translation (NLT)	New King James Version (NKJV)
28	Jacob's Dream at Bethel	Jacob's Dream at Bethel	Jacob Sent to His Uncle Laban
29	Jacob Arrives in Paddan Aram	Jacob Arrives in Paddan Aram	Jacob Marries Leah and Rachel
30	Jacob's Children	Jacob's Many Children	Jacob's Children
31	Jacob Flees from Laban	Jacob Flees from Laban	Jacob Leaves Laban
32	Jacob Prepares to Meet Esau		Jacob Prepares to Meet Esau
33	Jacob Meets Esau	Jacob and Esau Make Peace	Jacob and Esau Make Peace
34	Dinah and the Shechemites	Revenge Against Shechem	What Dinah's Brother Did
35	Jacob Returns to Bethel	Jacob Returns to Bethel	God Blesses Jacob at Bethel
36	Esau's Descendants	Descendants of Esau	The Family of Esau
37	Joseph's Dream	Joseph's Dream	Joseph's Dream
38	Judah and Tamar	Judah and Tamar	Sons of Judah

Prologue to the GPS Coordinates

Chapter	New International Version (NIV)	New Living Translation (NLT)	New King James Version (NKJV)
39	Joseph and Potiphar's Wife	Joseph in Potiphar's House	Joseph's Advancement
40	The Cupbearer and the Baker	Joseph Interprets Two Dreams	Joseph Interprets Dreams
41	Pharaoh's Dream	Pharaoh's Dream	Pharaoh's Dream
42	Joseph's Brothers Go to Egypt	Joseph's Brothers Go to Egypt	Joseph's Brothers Go to Egypt
43	The Second Journey to Egypt	The Brothers Return to Egypt	Joseph's Brothers Return with Benjamin
44	A Silver Cup in a Sack	Joseph's Silver Cup	Joseph's Final Test of His Brothers
45	Joseph Makes Himself Known	Joseph Reveals His Identity	Joseph Sends for Jacob
46	Jacob Goes to Egypt	Jacob's Journey to Egypt	Judah Pleads for His Brother Benjamin

His Majesty's Heavenly GPS

Chapter	New International Version (NIV)	New Living Translation (NLT)	New King James Version (NKJV)
47		Jacob Blesses Pharaoh	Joseph Is Governor of Egypt
48	Manasseh and Ephraim	Jacob Blesses Manasseh and Ephraim	Jacob Blesses Joseph's Sons
49	Jacob Blesses His Sons	Jacob's Last Words to His Sons	Jacob Prophecy Concerning His Sons
50			Burial of Jacob

CHAPTER 9

The Journey

This "GPS directives" of Genesis is the coming attraction set forth for the noble, extravagant, distinctive, specific protocol created for all mankind. Here you can experience the pain, laughter and joy of people who feel passionately like us, people whose temperaments operate in the psychological, emotional and spiritual realms like ours. People whose decisions altered the trajectory of their lives for better or worse. People who succeeded and those who failed. People whose hearts were broken and those called to heal the brokenness. We explore the cultural distinction, the varied forms of government, the institutions of learning, the medical advancements and the military strategies of ancient armies. We can view the infrastructures of cities and admire the beauty of their landscapes, much like the ones we appreciate even today.

Expand your horizons, choose the version of the Bible you prefer and snuggle up to this astonishing, amazing, true and profound script, filled with all the drama, suspense and action that your heart can absorb.

CHAPTER 10

Majestic Manual
Heavenly GPS Coordinates

As you read the "GPS directives" of Genesis, the specific keys listed below will assist in the comprehension of the style for which it was written. So we can better succeed as students of the Word, I pray that this formatted message will be impactful to the remembrance of the Scripture.

Book Key:

G—Genesis, Chapter and Verse

G 1/2:4 refers to Genesis—Chapter 1 and Chapter 2 Verse 4.

Example:
Dead End—denotes death.

Number before street—denotes the person's age at death.

127 Sarah Street—Sarah was 127 years old at time of death.

Example:
Left Turn—indicates the incorrect standard or decision-making process.

Right Turn—indicates the correct choice, decision-making, or clarity in conscious thought.

Begin at God's Purpose Path by the way of Creation Creek take ***G1/2:4***

His Majesty's Heavenly GPS

Turn left on Man Manor in the middle of Eden Lane *G2:7—G3*. Look for the Tree of Life and the Tree of Knowledge of Good and Evil in the center of Eden.

Proceed on *G4* to Birth Boulevard; pass Cain Creek and Abel Avenue.

Turn left on Cain Creek at the junction of Abel Avenue and 1st Murder Row.

Proceed to Nod Lane east of Eden Lane *G4:16* continue into the City of Enoch *G4:17*.

Go north on *G5* Adam's Avenue which leads you through Seth Street, Enoch Entrance, Methuselah Manor and Noah Nob.

As you approach Noah Nob *G6*, you will be adjacent to Flood Freeway *G7*. Take Flood Freeway to Rainbow Road *G8/9*.

Go south on *G9* to Covenant Center.

Continue south to *G10* until you reach the Tower of Babel Brook *G11*; observe Language Lane *G11:9* on the right from Shem Shore *G11:10* into Terah Terrance *G11:26* which becomes Abram Avenue, Nahor North and Haran Harbor.

Turn right on Abram Avenue *G12* and enter Blessings Boulevard *G12:1-3*.

Travel west by way of Sarai Street into Egypt Thruway.

Take Egypt Thruway north *G13* into Negev through Lot Lane.

Proceed on Lot Lane through Sodom Stroll and Gomorrah Gateway *G14* into Melchizedek Memorial Highway *G15*.

Continue on Melchizedek Memorial Highway *G15* into Covenant Crossing.

Majestic Manual: Heavenly GPS Coordinates

As you approach *G16*, you will see Ishmael Island. Proceed forward *G17* where Abram Avenue changes to Abraham Avenue (observe the change). Pass Circumcision Circle and continue on where Sarai Street becomes Sarah Street.

Take *G18* through Promise Passage, down Laughter Lane by way of Possibility Path.

Detour through Sodom City and Gomorrah Gateway *G19*. Pass Demolition Drive; exit to Gerar Grove *G20*.

Proceed on *G21* at Isaac and Ishmael Intersection; observe Faith Forest on the left and Obedience Orchard on the right until you see Provision Passage *G22*.

Make a sharp right turn at 127 Sarah Street, Kirjath Arba-Hebon, and Canaan where it ends *G23:1*. *(Dead End)*

Proceed to Abraham Avenue by way of Sons of Heth Heights into Ephron Elm at Silver Shekels Creek in Machpelah Cave County.

Continue on Mesopotamia Mills *G24:10-49*, along Servant at Camel Cove through Water Well between Laban Lot and Bethuel Bay *G24:50-61* to Isaac and Rebekah Junction. Observe Prayer Passage and Worship Way to Promise Place *G24:62-66*.

Adjacent to Promise Place, pass through Abraham Avenue which connects to Keturah Coast *G25* through the developments of Zimran, Joksahn Cove, Medan Mills, Midian Meadows, Ishbak Island and Shuah Site.

Make a sharp right turn at 175 Abraham Avenue, Kirjath Arba-Hebron, and Canaan where an end is *G25:7-8*. *(Dead End)*

Proceed down through Isaac and Ishmael Junction back to Machpelah Cave County *G25:9-10*.

After Dead End Drive, proceed to Isaac Estates on Blessings Boulevard *G25:11*.

Turn right on Families Freeway to Ishmael Island byway of Hagar Heights and Abraham Avenue. At Ishmael Island observe Nebajoth Nob, Kedar Creek, Mibsam Mill, Mishma Mill, Dumah, Massa Meadow, Hadar Hayes, Tema Trail, Jetur, Naphish Nob, and Kedemah Creek all on Sons Settlement *G25:12-16*.

Make a sharp right at 137 Ishmael Island east of Egypt where it ends *G25:17*. *(Dead End)*

Adjacent to Ishmael Island, return to Isaac and Rebekah Estates, pass Barren Lake into Conception Creek which observes Twin Towers at Esau Site next to Hairy Hunter Hall and Jacob Row next to Tent Trail *G25:19-27*.

Proceed through Esau Site and Jacob Row south to Birthright Boulevard. Turn left on Birthright Boulevard to Deception Drive *G25:29-34*.

Bear left on Water Rights Road until you see Oath Valley *G26*. Follow King Abimelech Alley through Gerar Grove to relocate the Isaac Estates. Observe Isaac Estates now located on Prosperity Passageway *G26:1-14*.

Continue through Prosperity Passageway into Philistines Port. Make a left turn at Denial District through Esek Well Way and Sitnah Well Harbor *G26:15-21*.

Make a right on Fruitful Shore into Rehoboth Well Region *G26:26:22*.

Take Oath Valley to Blessing Boulevard at Jacob Row and Esau Site Crossings *G27*.

Make a right onto Esau Site adjacent to Rebekah Hall into Deception Drive *G27:1-10*.

Follow Esau Site through Deception Drive to Blessing Boulevard arriving at the Isaac Estate *G27:21-40*.

Leaving Isaac Estate, make a left on Blessing Boulevard to Escape Freeway to Laban Lane *G27:41-45*.

Make right on Jacob's Ladder Landing, returning to Blessing Boulevard to Promise Place at Bethel Haven *G28:1-22*.

On Jacob Row, proceed toward Laban Lane to Rachel Road at 7th Walk Way and Deception Peak *G29:1-25*.

Return to 7th Walk Way and Rachel Road until you arrive at Reward Grove *G29:27-30*.

Proceed to Leah-Rachel Intersection into Rachel Road at Barren Bridge and Leah Creek at Fruitful Shore *G29:31*.

Follow Leah Heights through Conception Court to Reuben Region, Simeon Summit, Levi Loop and Judah Jubilee *G29:32-35*.

Pass Conception Court over Barren Bridge to Rachel Road. On Rachel Road, observe Bilhah Maiden Bay on the left of Conception Court into the developments of the District of Dan and Naphtali North *G30:1-8*.

Make a left off of Rachel Road into Leah Heights. Follow Leah Heights to Zilpah Maiden Bay on the left of Conception Court into the developments of Gad Grove and Asher Alley *G30:9-13*.

Continue on Leah Heights through Conception Court into the developments of Issachar Island, Zebulun Trail and Dinah Meadows *G30:17-21*.

At Conception Court, make a right on Rachel Road until you see Joseph's Freeway *G30:22-24*.

After Joseph's Freeway, turn right at Jacob Row then proceed to Laban Lane adjacent to Increase Island *G30:25-43*.

At Increase Island observe Grumble Grove and Attitude Alley at Laban Lounge and Son Center *G31:1-2*.

Proceed to Canaan Crossing, over Euphrates River through Gilead Gateway *G31:3-20.*

Make a left on Gilead Gateway and intersect at Laban Lane to Accusation Alley *G31:22-30.*

Follow Accusation Alley onto Rachel Road and Household Gods Grove *G31:31-42.*

Make a right on Treaty Thruway toward Witness Pile Passage and Mizpah Mill *G31:52.*

Merge onto Oath Court by way of Boundary Boulevard at Laban Lane and Jacob Row *G31:53-55.*

Take Jacob Row to Mahanaim Manor and Angelic Avenue. Exit Seir Street toward Edom Expressway/Esau Freeway *G32:1-3.*

Turn right on Esau Freeway onto Prayer Place through Jacob Row *G32:4-12.*

Take Jacob Row to Gift Gate/Forgiveness Fort toward Esau Freeway *G32:13-21.*

Proceed on Jacob Row at the intersection of Wrestle Way (Jacob Row becomes Israel Expressway) *G32:21-29.*

Merge onto Esau Freeway to Reconciliation Highway *G33.*

Turn left at Shechem Stroll onto Dinah Drive at Defiled Way *G34:1-5.*

Turn left onto Hamor Place adjacent to Shechem Stroll and Brothers Byway next to Dinah Drive *G34:6-12.*

Take the Shechem Stroll to Deception Turnpike toward Slaughter Strait *G34:13-29.*

Turn left on Slaughter Strait and make a sharp right on Bethel Boulevard. Observe Deborah Passage *G35:1-8. (Dead End)*

Majestic Manual: Heavenly GPS Coordinates

Proceed on Bethel Boulevard to Bethlehem Boulevard until you reach Benjamin Estates. Make a sharp left onto Rachel Road *G35:16-20*. *(Dead End)*

Turn right at Jacob Row into Hebron Hollow. Observe 180 Isaac *G35:27-28*. *(Dead End)*

Merge onto Esau Expressway to Joseph Interstate. Make a left on Dream Crossroad adjacent to Slavery Pathway *G37*.

Come to Judah/Tamar Junction. Make a left on Judah/Tamar Junction *G38*.

Merge back to Joseph Interstate. Exit left on Potiphar Place *G39*.

Turn left on Prison Path *G39:19-23*.

Follow Prison Path through Dream Concourse past Cupbearer Creek and Baker's Lane *G40*.

Continue along Joseph Interstate. Turn right at Pharaoh Palace through Dream Conduit. Proceed to Provision Place *G41*.

Merge at Provision Place onto Brothers Brook toward Famine Forest *G42 – 43*.

Make a right turn onto Strategy Circle *G44*.

Turn right on Identity Island *G45:1-6*.

Make a right into Forgiveness Freeway *G45:7-8*.

Turn right on Restoration Road *G45:9-28*.

Proceed on Restoration Road to Jacob Row. Take Jacob Row to Goshen Gateway *G46*.

Follow Goshen Gateway to Egypt Estates, by way of Jacob Row to Pharaoh Palace *G47:1-10*.

His Majesty's Heavenly GPS

Proceed to Joseph Interstate by way of Jacob Row to Manasseh Manor and Ephraim Trail *G48.*

Continue on Jacob Row to 12 Son Blessing Place. Observe 147 Jacob Row *G49. (Dead End)*

Merge back on Joseph Interstate Exit 50 toward Reassurance Walk *G50:14-21.*

Turn right on Reassurance Walk. Observe Joseph Interstate 110 *G50:22-26. (Dead End)*

As we continue this divine excursion and this magnificent journey, join me in exploring His Majesty's MapQuest—Volume 2—The Crescendo of Creativity.

CHAPTER 11

GOD COMMANDED THE HISTORY OF CREATION

Everything that came into manifestation was spoken and created by the King of Kings. You can see by the following graphic representations how God created all things by the spoken word and then named and blessed what He made.

REFERENCES FROM THE BOOK OF GENESIS		
God Created	God Said	God Saw
1:1	1:3	1:4
1:21	1:6	1:12
1:27	1:9	1:18
	1:11	1:21
	1:14	1:25
	1:20	1:31
	1:24	
	1:26	
	1:28	
	1:29	

His Majesty's Heavenly GPS

God Called	According to Its Kind	Various
1:5 (Twice)	1:11	1:4 – God divided
1:8	1:12 (Twice)	1:7 – God made
1:10 (Twice)	1:21 (Twice)	1:16 – God made (Twice)
	1:24 (Twice)	1:17 – God set
	1:25 (Three Times)	1:22 – God blessed
		1:25 – God made
		1:28 – God blessed
		1:31 – He had made

WE ARE GRATEFUL

You caused us to boldly step into the declaration of our divine destiny and proclaim, announce and echo the promises for the inevitable presence. You align our hearts with the clarion call of a defining moment set forth by the hand of the Creator of the universe. We are grateful to be partakers of this magnificent, brilliant, creative, extraordinary, supernatural, uncommon life with which You have endowed us. We are thankful that You designed us with such purpose, dimension and determination to pursue that for which we have been called. The call is glorious. The assignment is tedious. But the intention is perfectly aligned with Your will. Therefore, we shall go forth and do ALL You have designed, ordained, created and set forth for us to accomplish.

Neither fortune or fame, nor riches or wealth, nor influence, nor affluence, nor relations, nor resources or lack of resources can stop the curtains of death from unveiling the end of an era, season, person, or promise. The God of the Universe, the Omniscient God, who so perfectly, lovingly, and sovereignly began it all shall surely end it. The One who spoke the Words of Life for the manifestation of a world unknown shall speak a Word of benediction over all creation.

ROYAL DECREES

CREATION AND CREATURES APPLAUD YOU, GOD;
YOUR HOLY PEOPLE BLESS YOU.
THEY TALK ABOUT THE GLORIES OF YOUR RULE,
THEY EXCLAIM OVER YOUR SPLENDOR,

PSALMS 145:10–11

THIS IS THE HISTORY OF [THE ORIGIN OF] THE HEAVENS AND OF THE EARTH WHEN THEY WERE CREATED, IN THE DAY [THAT IS, DAYS OF CREATION] THAT THE LORD GOD MADE THE EARTH AND THE HEAVENS.

GENESIS 2:4 (AMP)

"AT THE BEGINNING YOU FOUNDED THE EARTH;
THE HEAVENS ARE THE WORK OF YOUR HANDS."

PSALMS 102:25 (AMP)

DO WHAT GOD TELLS YOU. WALK IN THE PATHS HE SHOWS YOU: FOLLOW THE LIFE-MAP ABSOLUTELY, KEEP AN EYE OUT FOR THE SIGNPOSTS, HIS COURSE FOR LIFE SET OUT IN THE REVELATION TO MOSES; THEN YOU'LL GET ON WELL IN WHATEVER YOU DO AND WHEREVER YOU GO.

1 KINGS 2:3

His Majesty's Heavenly GPS

ROYAL DECREES

THE REVELATION OF GOD IS WHOLE
AND PULLS OUR LIVES TOGETHER.
THE SIGNPOSTS OF GOD ARE CLEAR
AND POINT OUT THE RIGHT ROAD.
THE LIFE-MAPS OF GOD ARE RIGHT,
SHOWING THE WAY TO JOY.
THE DIRECTIONS OF GOD ARE PLAIN
AND EASY ON THE EYES.
GOD'S REPUTATION IS TWENTY-FOUR-CARAT
GOLD, WITH A LIFETIME GUARANTEE.
THE DECISIONS OF GOD ARE ACCURATE
DOWN TO THE NTH DEGREE.

PSALMS 19:7–9

THE VERY STEPS WE TAKE COME FROM GOD;
OTHERWISE HOW WOULD WE KNOW WHERE
WE'RE GOING?

PROVERBS 20:24

MARK WELL THAT GOD DOESN'T MISS A MOVE YOU
MAKE; HE'S AWARE OF EVERY STEP YOU TAKE.

PROVERBS 5:21

ROYAL DECREES

O LORD, HOW MANY AND VARIED ARE YOUR WORKS!
IN WISDOM YOU HAVE MADE THEM ALL;
THE EARTH IS FULL OF YOUR RICHES AND YOUR
CREATURES. THERE IS THE SEA, GREAT AND BROAD,
IN WHICH ARE SWARMS WITHOUT NUMBER,
CREATURES BOTH SMALL AND GREAT.
THERE THE SHIPS [OF THE SEA] SAIL, AND LEVIATHAN
[THE SEA MONSTER], WHICH YOU HAVE FORMED TO PLAY
THERE. THEY ALL WAIT FOR YOU TO GIVE THEM THEIR
FOOD IN ITS APPOINTED SEASON. YOU GIVE IT TO THEM,
THEY GATHER IT UP; YOU OPEN YOUR HAND, THEY ARE
FILLED AND SATISFIED WITH GOOD [THINGS].
YOU HIDE YOUR FACE, THEY ARE DISMAYED;
YOU TAKE AWAY THEIR BREATH, THEY DIE
AND RETURN TO THEIR DUST.
YOU SEND OUT YOUR SPIRIT, THEY ARE CREATED;
YOU RENEW THE FACE OF THE GROUND.

PSALMS 104:24–30 (AMP)

WHAT A WILDLY WONDERFUL WORLD, GOD!
YOU MADE IT ALL, WITH WISDOM AT YOUR SIDE,
MADE EARTH OVERFLOW WITH YOUR WONDERFUL
CREATION.

PSALMS 104:24

His Majesty's Heavenly GPS

ROYAL DECREES

FOR THE VERY STRUCTURES OF EARTH ARE GOD'S;
HE HAS LAID OUT HIS OPERATIONS ON A FIRM
FOUNDATION.

1 SAMUEL 2:8

GOD'S GLORY IS ON TOUR IN THE SKIES,
GOD-CRAFT ON EXHIBIT ACROSS THE HORIZON.
MADAME DAY HOLDS CLASSES EVERY MORNING,
PROFESSOR NIGHT LECTURES EACH EVENING.
THEIR WORDS AREN'T HEARD,
THEIR VOICES AREN'T RECORDED,
BUT THEIR SILENCE FILLS THE EARTH:
UNSPOKEN TRUTH IS SPOKEN EVERYWHERE.

PSALMS 19:1–5

BLESS GOD, ALL CREATURES, WHEREVER YOU ARE—
EVERYTHING AND EVERYONE MADE BY GOD.

PSALMS 103:22

KNOW THAT THE LORD, HE IS GOD;
IT IS HE WHO HAS MADE US, AND NOT WE OURSELVES.

PSALMS 100:3 (NKJV)

ROYAL DECREES

BLESS GOD, ALL CREATURES, WHEREVER YOU ARE—
EVERYTHING AND EVERYONE MADE BY GOD.

PSALMS 103:22

GOD CLAIMS EARTH AND EVERYTHING IN IT, GOD
CLAIMS WORLD AND ALL WHO LIVE ON IT.
HE BUILT IT ON OCEAN FOUNDATIONS, LAID IT
OUT ON RIVER GIRDERS.

PSALMS 24:1–2

BE GENEROUS WITH ME AND I'LL LIVE A FULL
LIFE; NOT FOR A MINUTE WILL I TAKE MY EYES OFF
YOUR ROAD. OPEN MY EYES SO I CAN SEE WHAT YOU
SHOW ME OF YOUR MIRACLE-WONDERS.
I'M A STRANGER IN THESE PARTS;
GIVE ME CLEAR DIRECTIONS.

PSALMS 119:17–19

KEEP YOUR EYES OPEN FOR GOD, WATCH FOR HIS
WORKS; BE ALERT FOR SIGNS OF HIS PRESENCE.
REMEMBER THE WORLD OF WONDERS HE HAS MADE,
HIS MIRACLES, AND THE VERDICTS HE'S RENDERED.

PSALMS 105:5

His Majesty's Heavenly GPS

ROYAL DECREES

O MY SOUL, BLESS GOD!
GOD, MY GOD, HOW GREAT YOU ARE!
BEAUTIFULLY, GLORIOUSLY ROBED,
DRESSED UP IN SUNSHINE, AND ALL HEAVEN STRETCHED
OUT FOR YOUR TENT. YOU BUILT YOUR PALACE ON THE
OCEAN DEEPS, MADE A CHARIOT OUT OF CLOUDS AND
TOOK OFF ON WIND-WINGS.
YOU COMMANDEERED WINDS AS MESSENGERS,
APPOINTED FIRE AND FLAME AS AMBASSADORS.
YOU SET EARTH ON A FIRM FOUNDATION SO THAT
NOTHING CAN SHAKE IT, EVER.
YOU BLANKETED EARTH WITH OCEAN,
COVERED THE MOUNTAINS WITH DEEP WATERS;
THEN YOU ROARED AND THE WATER RAN AWAY—
YOUR THUNDER CRASH PUT IT TO FLIGHT.
MOUNTAINS PUSHED UP, VALLEYS SPREAD OUT IN THE
PLACES YOU ASSIGNED THEM.
YOU SET BOUNDARIES BETWEEN EARTH AND SEA;
NEVER AGAIN WILL EARTH BE FLOODED.
YOU STARTED THE SPRINGS AND RIVERS, SENT THEM
FLOWING AMONG THE HILLS.
ALL THE WILD ANIMALS NOW DRINK THEIR FILL,
WILD DONKEYS QUENCH THEIR THIRST.
ALONG THE RIVERBANKS THE BIRDS BUILD NESTS,
RAVENS MAKE THEIR VOICES HEARD.
YOU WATER THE MOUNTAINS FROM YOUR HEAVENLY
CISTERNS;
EARTH IS SUPPLIED WITH PLENTY OF WATER.
YOU MAKE GRASS GROW FOR THE LIVESTOCK,
HAY FOR THE ANIMALS THAT PLOW THE GROUND.

PSALM 104:1–14

ROYAL DECREES

HE'S GOD, OUR GOD,
IN CHARGE OF THE WHOLE EARTH. AND HE
REMEMBERS, REMEMBERS HIS COVENANT—FOR
A THOUSAND GENERATIONS HE'S BEEN
AS GOOD AS HIS WORD.

PSALMS 105:7

Royal Names

Yahweh-'asah / The Lord our Maker	Psalms 95:6
El / The strong and mighty One, the all-sufficient Creator	Genesis 35:11
Elohim / God, the strong and mighty One; the first name of God in Scripture	Genesis 1:1
El-elyon / The Most High God	Genesis 14:19
El-shaddai / God Almighty, the breasted One	Genesis 17:1
El-roi / God, the all-seeing, watchful One	Genesis 16:13
El-olam / The everlasting God	Genesis 21:33
El-bethel / God of the house of God	Genesis 28:18–19
Yahweh-ga'al / The Lord your Redeemer	Isaiah 54:8
Elohim-kol'erets / The God of the whole earth	Isaiah 54:5
El-de'ah / The God of knowledge	1 Samuel 2:3
El-'emeth / The God of truth	Psalms 31:5
El-shamayim / The God of heaven	Psalms 136:26

His Majesty's Heavenly GPS

I am particularly grateful for, my mentors coach, manager and prayer partners who have believed in me and the vision God has set before me.

With—

Faith on the Freeway
Perseverance on the Platform
Blessings on the Boulevard
Joy on the Journey
Gratitude through the Thoroughfare
Belief on the Boardwalk
Possibilities in the Park
Desire at the Doorpost
Strength on the Street
Favor on the Freeway
God as our General

Being led by the Holy Spirit Tour Guide, we remain on the uncompromising righteous course.

We have Soared in our Social Capital!
We have Developed our Digital Footprints!
We have Amplified our Audio Voiceprint!
We have Maximized our Mental Image!

We will successfully complete the journey, not with perfection, but with perseverance, and the truth is—We win, now and forevermore!

Royal Names

FINAL ROYAL DECREE

TO YOU, O GOD, BELONG THE GREATNESS AND THE
MIGHT, THE GLORY, THE VICTORY, THE MAJESTY, THE
SPLENDOR; YES! EVERYTHING IN HEAVEN, EVERYTHING
ON EARTH; THE KINGDOM ALL YOURS!
YOU'VE RAISED YOURSELF HIGH OVER ALL.
RICHES AND GLORY COME FROM YOU.
YOU'RE RULER OVER ALL;
YOU HOLD STRENGTH AND POWER IN THE PALM OF
YOUR HAND TO BUILD UP AND STRENGTHEN ALL.
AND HERE WE ARE, O GOD, OUR GOD, GIVING THANKS
TO YOU, PRAISING YOUR SPLENDID NAME.

1 CHRONICLES 29:11–13

The Golden Touch of His Beauty

The golden touch of His beauty beacons to you—Come!
Come and be refreshed at the fountain of My love.
Come and be renewed in the garden of My glory.
Come and be restored by the brook of My blessing—Come!
Come and be revived by the wind of My wonders,
The pleasure of My peace,
The jubilance of My joy,
The essence of My embrace—Come!!!
Everything I have is at your disposal awaiting the release
of the genius into you before your breath exhaled
into the atmosphere
or your eyes beheld the loveliness of a cascading sky.
The genius that whispers to your intellect or empowers
you to sing unheard melodies;
The genius that masterminded your imagination so
that creativity takes flight;
The genius that provokes you to love the image of yourself
before the portrait is complete;
The genius that separates your hearing from your listening,
Your understanding from your comprehension,
And your knowledge from your wisdom.
All of this amazing genius, I endowed you with before you
ever knew your name.
You are the premier craftsmanship of My unlimited,
unconditional, boundless love.
You need not search any further—the treasure is YOU!!!
Every precious jewel meticulously arranged to express the
magnificence of YOU!
An exquisite gift packaged for an amazing world.
A world awaiting the piece of the life's puzzle
completing divine destiny.
It is the "Golden Touch of His Beauty" which
conducted the symphony of your soul.
As it resounded with original, unique, matchless—YOU!!!

Acknowledgments

First I acknowledge my precious Lord and Savior, Jesus Christ, whose breath of life resurrected me and caused me to LIVE!

Second, I acknowledge the following dear people God has used to profoundly impact my life:

Virginia Brown Harvey, my mom, an extraordinarily creative, loving, wise, orphan woman, who showed me how to be a woman of wisdom, prosperity and grace.

Herbert Shaw Clemons, my husband, a man seeking God's heart, intellectual genius and gifted forgiver who has shown me that adversities of life have no power over perseverance, love, and the desire to win.

Willie Leroy Harvey (deceased) my hilarious, funny, comedic father, who demonstrated that authenticity is the key to freedom. Be who you are and be ready for the rewards and the consequences.

Chalet A. (Tranumn) Jean-Baptiste my precious, phenomenal, benevolent, loving daughter, whose trials, tests, monumental accomplishments, tenacity and extraordinary faith sustained, expanded and enhanced my devout trust in God.

Ariana Tranumn, **Christophe**r and **Elise Jean Baptiste**, my cherish, loving, kindhearted, blessed grandchildren who bring me joy unspeakable.

Beulah Bunnell Grandy, my great aunt, a Holy Spirit-filled, devoted Kingdom Ambassador and her husband, **Rayfield Grandy** ("Big Daddy") (both deceased) who raised me in the reverential fear of the Lord that incubated within me spiritual roots and moral character for a lifetime.

Acknowledgments

Sarah Wilson-Gordon (deceased) and **Leatrice Grandy-Williams**, my adopted sisters/cousins, whose protection, love, encouragement and understanding kept me focused and gave me strength through the years we were raised together.

In memory of the hard working, integral, honest, steadfastness and resilience of my mother's sisters:

- **Willie Mae Brown**
- **Gladys Brown Sivels**
- **Gracie Brown Rogers**
- **Doris Brown Davis**

who all taught me to be strong and NEVER quit.

For the lovingkindness of my father, Willie Leroy Harvey's, family:

- **Great-grandmother, Dorothy Wilson** (aka; Mama Dot) – a fountain of love that never ran dry for 102 years and a supernatural prayer warrior.
- **Grandma - Carrie Wilson**, an exemplary businesswoman implanted within us that "Family is everything."
- **My sweet Aunt Annie** who declared that I was her "first baby" and loved me unselfishly.
- **Uncle Hubert Jr.** (aka **Rev. Dr. Hubert Wilson, Jr.**) a Holy Ghost Pastor with a heart of gold for all he encountered who are in need. A Spirit-filled, mighty man of God with untiring love, peace and generosity.
- **Aunt Carol (Jose)** whose home was always mine, day or night. Food ready to eat and car were willing to go—wherever desired.
- **Uncle Woodrow** whose laughter and dedication filled my heart with joy reminding me that LOVE has no distance or time.

Acknowledgments

For my gracious, compassionate, kind and loving in-laws:

• **Johnnie Mae Clemons** (deceased), my mother-in-law, a sweet, caring woman who always considered me a daughter.

• **Deloris Williams** (deceased) sister-in-law and very best friend, in whom I confidentially shared my life without any concern of judgement. Her love was infectious.

- **Marion Granison**
- **Cynthia Clemons** with her heart of laughter.
- **Cecilia Clemons**, the concerned sister with a kind heart.
- **Olivia Clemons**, the strong sister with a gentle heart.
- **Jeanette Clemons**, the baby girl with the sweetest heart.
- **Tony Clemons**
- **Selvyn Clemons**

For my adopted brother and sister, Ted and Karen Gustus, whose love and support carried me through the storm and rejoiced with me on the mountain top. Thanks for always being there. I am so grateful. Thanks for the encouragement, coaching, motivation, and enthusiasm expressed for my dreams.

For my mentors and dedicated friends, prophetic, apostolic voices to the nations, Apostle Prophets Martin and Michelle Johnson, whose prophetic instructions, mentorship and unwavering prayers and intercession transformed my life with deeper revelation and inspiring conviction.

For my former pastor (25 years), Dr. A.R. Bernard, Sr., Senior Pastor of New York Christian Cultural Centre, a prolific teacher of the Gospel of Jesus Christ, a man of wisdom and valor who instilled and fortified within me the practical application of the Word of God.

- **Deborah Perry**, my confidant and precious friend, who ingrained in me the expression "But, what does the Word of God say?" Thanks so very much.

Acknowledgments

- **Lucille Nichols** and **Famous Rogers**, remarkable, accomplished, thoughtful cousins.
- **Priscilla Storey**, devoted, loyal and committed friend whose care and support continually covered me.
- **Celeste Rivers**, a friend who gives her all with unrestrained sacrifice.
- **Howard J. Tranumn, Jr.**, good-natured, respected, confidant and friend.
- **Apostle Patricia Rodgers-Wiley**, encourager, prophet and adopted sister who always cherished the gift of God in me, a tenderhearted nurturer to my daughter.
- **Wesley Wiley**, my superb vocal coach, a renowned singer, composer, musician, preacher and evangelist.

I appreciate the benevolent, unwavering friendship of:

- **Thelma Martin** (deceased)
- **Cynthelia McIntosh**
- **Carol Turesky Gordon**
- **Deborah (Slater) Licorish**
- **Darquette Robinson**
- **Mother Ella Kelly**
- **Vic and Kathy Lee**
- **Dorian Owens** – talented, ingenious photographer.

My heart goes out to my amazing spiritual daughters/sons:

- **Khiem Reed**
- **Melinda and Johnathan Brundidge**
- **Darwin and Traci Hobbs**

Acknowledgments

Some of my greatest inspirational leaders and influencers of all times:

- **Jim and Mary Kocher**, Primerica Financial Services, friends and business persons extraordinaire.
- **Principal Gregory Coleman** (deceased), an encourager who caused me to soar (John M. Coleman JHS, Brooklyn, New York).
- **Dr. Cindy Trimm**, gracious mentor, coach and prolific teacher.
- **Foster Scott** (deceased) teacher (Crestwood High School Chesapeake, Va.) who taught me to believe in myself.
- **Media Whitehurst and Tootsie Bryant**, who birthed me into my gift of song.

Special thanks to my manager, **Melinda Brundidge**, an administrative genius whose compassion, kindness and detail for precision and excellence sustained me through this literary process.

And finally, deep appreciation for my pastors, **Pastors Ashley and Jane Evans**, Influencer's Church of Atlanta (Gwinnett Campus), whose global commitment to share the love of Jesus Christ to every nation, ethnicity has propelled me to spiritual heights unforeseen.

Because of the influence of these dear people, today, "I am a Kingdom Subject."

ENDNOTES

[1] Eugene H. Peterson, *The Message Bible: The Old Testament Books of Moses*, First Edition, Copyright ©2001 by Navpress Pub Group. Quote taken from page 19.

[2] GPS, https://dictionary.cambridge.org/us/dictionary/English/gps, page 1, accessed September 16, 2019.

[3] John Maxwell, *The Maxwell Leadership Bible*, Second Edition, Copyright ©2002, 2007 by Maxwell Motivation, Inc. and Tim Elmore, Executive Editors. The Holy Bible, New King James Version Copyright © 1982 by Thomas Nelson, Inc. Thomas Nelson Publishers. Quote taken from page 665 – Introduction To Psalms – God's Role in Psalms.

[4] Sunset Travellers, "*30 Best Handpicked Sunset Quotes That Will Inspire You.*" Accessed February 11, 2019, https://sunsettravellers.com/sunset-quotes.

[5] Myles Monroe, *The Glory Living, Keys to Releasing Your Personal Glory* (Shippensburg, PA, Destiny Image Publishers, Inc. 2005) page 23.

PEGGY CLEMONS / EXTENDED BIO

Peggy Clemons was born in Virginia Beach, Virginia. She is a speaker, singer and actress. For over four decades, Peggy has inspired others and has been recognized for her multi-faceted talents along the way. For example, one of many awards includes the "Woman History Maker" recognition from Brooklyn Borough President in 1999.

As an accomplished singer for 45 years and actress for 42 years, Peggy has performed at world-renowned venues such as Carnegie Hall and Madison Square Garden in New York City (NYC), the United States Capitol for the National Campaign to Stop Violence, and the Apollo Theater in NYC. She was the opening act for musical legend Shirley Caesar, performed with a 150-piece orchestra, and sang for audiences of over 30,000 people. Additionally, Peggy has graced the stage with Alvin Ailey's dance legend, Judith Jamison, and performed on Broadway as the lead vocalist for the production "Mama, I Want to Sing." Peggy's experience runs the gamut as she has performed all over the Unites States, on television and she's performed before national dignitaries such as former First Lady, Hillary Clinton.

Alongside Peggy's career in entertainment, she spent 40 years as a passionate educator and public speaker. During her span in education, Peggy served as an Assistant Principal, School Administrator, Physical Education Teacher, Guidance Counselor, Dance Instructor, Choreographer, and Choir Director where she received many accolades including "Outstanding Teacher of the Year" and "Outstanding Guidance Counselor of the Year" awards in New York City. In November 2016, Peggy received the Obama Presidential Lifetime Achievement Award for lifetime commitment to building a stronger nation through volunteer services.

On November 12, 2017, she also was ordained by Dr. Cindy Trimm into Cindy Trimm Ministries International, Inc. as a member of the Global Alliance of Christian Leaders at the Georgia World Congress Center. Over the years, she has honed her gift to motivate and encourage others and has become a sought-after speaker and leader.

Being a life-long learner, Peggy earned her Bachelor's, Master's and post Master's degrees from Long Island University and City University of New York respectively. She now is a member of Influencers Church of Atlanta under the awesome and dynamic leadership of Pastors Ashley and Jane Evans, and serves as one of the leaders of the Prayer and Intercession Team.

Peggy is the loving daughter and caretaker of Virginia Harvey, her greatest friend, role model and confidant. She currently resides in Oxford, Georgia, with her husband Herb Clemons of 32 years and is the mother of one daughter and grandmother of three.

MISS PEGGY SINGING AT THE MISS BROOKLYN PAGEANT JULY 13, 1974